EDGE
BOOKS™

HOW TO DRAW
ELVES,
DWARVES,
AND OTHER MAGICAL FOLK

BY AJ SAUTTER
FEATURING 5 ARTISTS

CAPSTONE PRESS
a capstone imprint

Edge Books are published by Capstone Press,
1710 Roe Crest Drive, North Mankato, Minnesota 56003
www.mycapstone.com

Library of Congress Cataloging-in-Publication Data
Sautter, Aaron, author.
How to draw elves, dwarves, and other magical folk / by A.J. Sautter.
pages cm.—(Edge books. Drawing fantasy creatures)
Includes bibliographical references.
Summary: "Simple, step-by-step instructions teach readers how to draw elves, dwarves,
and several other magical fantasy creatures"—Provided by publisher.
ISBN 978-1-4914-8027-4 (library binding)
ISBN 978-1-4914-8410-4 (eBook PDF)
1. Fairies in art—Juvenile literature. 2. Elves in art—Juvenile literature.
3. Drawing—Technique—Juvenile literature. I. Title.
NC825.F22S28 2016
743'.87—dc23   2015026183

Editorial Credits
Kyle Grenz, designer; Kelly Garvin, media researcher; Gene Bentdahl, production specialist

Illustration Credits
Capstone Press: Colin Howard, cover, 1, 6-7, 12-13, 14-15, Jason Juta, cover, 1, 22-23,
26-27, Martin Bustamante, cover, 1, 20-21, 28-31, Stefano Azzalin, cover, back cover, 1,
8-9, 10-11, 16-17, 24-25, Tom McGrath, cover, 1, 18-19

Design Elements
Capstone Press; Shutterstock: aopsan, Bambuh, blue pencil, Kompaniets,
Marta Jonina, Molodec, val lawless

Printed in the United States of America, in North Mankato Minnesota.
092015   009221CGS16

TABLE OF CONTENTS

DRAWING MAGICAL PEOPLE

Have you ever been walking in the woods and noticed something moving at the corner of your eye? Maybe it was just a squirrel or chipmunk running behind a tree. But with a little imagination, it could be something magical. Perhaps it was a fairy, a gnome, or a satyr hiding in the shadows.

If you have an active imagination you may enjoy drawing fantastic magical creatures. If so, then this book is for you! Grab some paper and pencils and get ready to set your imagination free. First follow the drawing steps in each project to begin sketching elves, dwarves, merfolk, and other magical beings. After practicing them a few times, try drawing them in different poses or settings. You can even create scenes of your favorite characters facing dangerous fantasy monsters. Then when your art is ready, you can color it. There are many ways to color your creations, including colored pencils, markers, and paint. Just let your inner artist be your guide!

FINDING YOUR STYLE

Don't worry if your drawings aren't exactly like those you see in this book. Every artist has his or her own style. If you keep practicing, your own art style will develop over time. Soon you'll be creating awesome creatures and fantasy artwork of your very own.

GATHER YOUR SUPPLIES

Before you can start drawing, you'll need to gather some basic supplies. With the following materials in hand, you'll be ready to sketch anything your imagination can create.

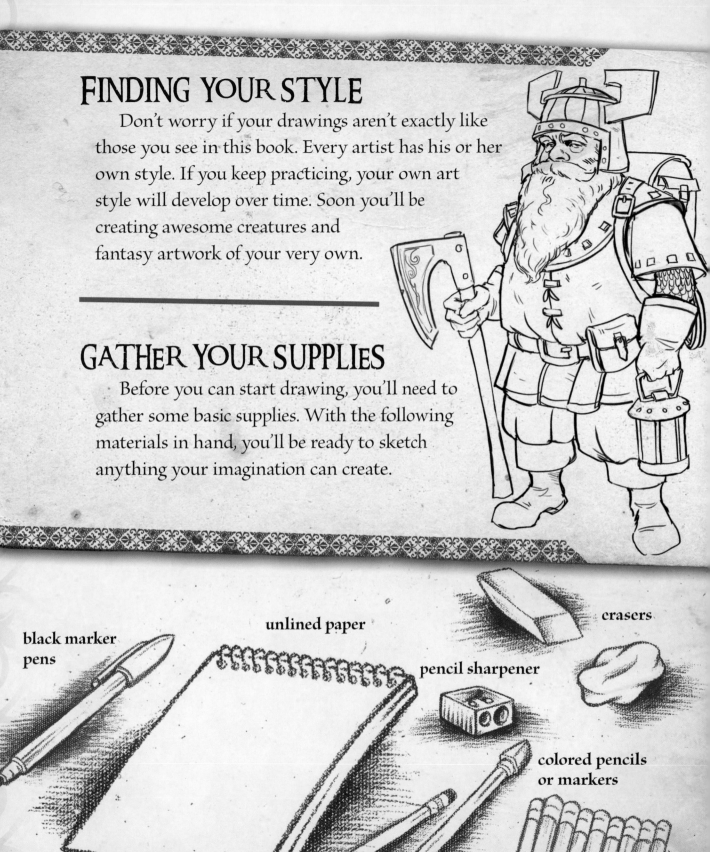

black marker pens

unlined paper

erasers

pencil sharpener

colored pencils or markers

sharp pencils

CENTAURS

Centaurs are proud creatures and normally keep to themselves. They rarely make friends with outsiders. However, centaurs are extremely loyal to the few friends they do have. They will gladly risk their lives to help friends in need. Centaurs are also very skilled with bows, swords, and other weapons and are deadly during a fight.

SIZE: ABOUT 7 TO 7.5 FEET (2.1 TO 2.3 METERS) TALL

HABITAT: FORESTS, PLAINS, AND FOOTHILLS NEAR MOUNTAINS

Physical Features: Centaurs are part human and part horse. Their human upper bodies are strong and muscular. They usually have long, flowing hair, and some males also grow bushy beards. Centaurs' powerful, horselike lower bodies are usually covered in dark brown or black hair.

1

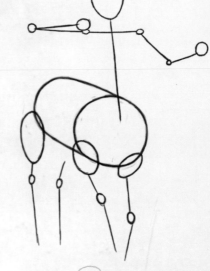

2

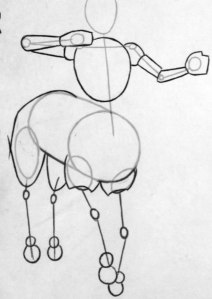

3

4

5

FINAL

WHAT'S NEXT?

When you've finished drawing
this centaur, try drawing another
rearing up on its hind legs or
fighting an enemy with an axe.

SATYRS

Satyrs love a good party and having fun with their friends. They also love nature and enjoy exploring forests. Most satyrs are also skilled musicians. They often play panpipes to cast magic musical spells to entertain their friends. Satyrs may also use their musical spells to confuse enemies or put them to sleep.

SIZE: ABOUT 5 TO 5.5 FEET (1.5 TO 1.7 M) TALL

HABITAT: THICK FORESTS AND HILLY REGIONS NEAR MOUNTAINS

Physical Features: Satyrs have legs and feet like goats and upper bodies similar to humans. Their heads and faces combine both human and goatlike features. They have long, narrow noses and large, curved horns. Many satyrs also have beardlike whiskers growing from their chins.

1

2

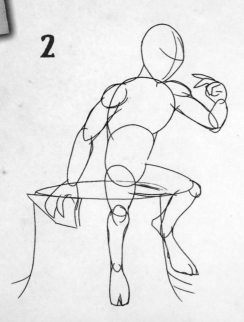

3

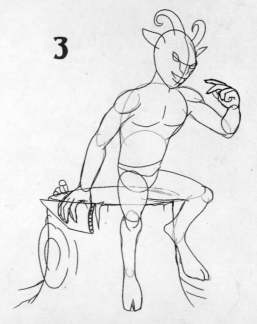

4

5

FINAL

WHAT'S NEXT?

Practice drawing this satyr a few times, then try drawing several of them dancing and playing music in a forest clearing.

FAIRIES

Fairies usually use their magical form to hide their true appearance. They are very curious and like to explore the world. Fairies are often friendly, talkative, and outgoing. However, they are easily angered by people who harm the natural world. They'll use their magic to scare off anyone they feel is a threat.

SIZE: IN MAGICAL FORM: THE SIZE OF LARGE BUTTERFLIES OR OTHER WINGED INSECTS

HABITAT: WOODLAND AREAS FILLED WITH STREAMS AND MEADOWS

Physical Features: In magical form fairies appear as butterflies, moths, dragonflies, and other flying insects. But in their true form they appear as beautiful young women. Fairies are best known for the large, lightweight wings attached to their backs.

1

2

3

4

5

FINAL

WHAT'S NEXT?

Now try drawing another fairy
flying by some flowers. Give
her some different clothing or
some different colorful wings.

BROWNIES

Brownies like to stay hidden, but they are very friendly. They often do household chores during the night, such as mending clothes, cleaning dishes, and mopping floors. Brownies never expect any payment. But they can be easily insulted if someone criticizes their work. They may hide important items or make large messes to get back at those who offended them.

SIZE: ABOUT 8 TO 12 INCHES (20 TO 30 CENTIMETERS) TALL

HABITAT: CRAWL SPACES, ATTICS, AND OTHER SMALL SPACES IN BARNS AND FARMHOUSES

Physical Features: Brownies are short creatures that appear somewhat ratlike. They have beady black eyes, pointed ears and noses, whiskers, and strong front teeth. Brownies usually wear shabby clothes made from scraps of cloth that they find while doing their work.

1

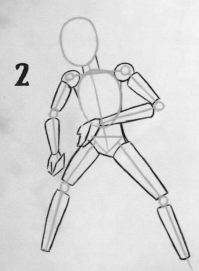

2

3

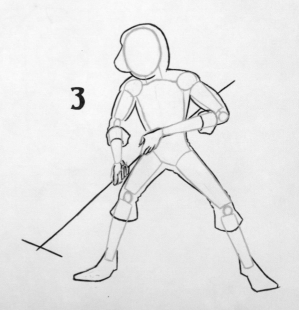

4

5

FINAL

WHAT'S NEXT?

After drawing this brownie, try drawing him in his living space with buttons, pins, and other small items he's collected.

GNOMES

Gnomes often seem gruff and unfriendly toward strangers. But they usually mean no harm. They simply prefer a peaceful life and little contact with outsiders. Gnomes spend most of their time gathering food or mining for gems underground. They are also skilled craftsmen. Their jewelry is often considered some of the finest in the world.

SIZE: ABOUT 18 TO 24 INCHES (46 TO 61 CM) TALL

HABITAT: SMALL CAVES AND HOLLOW TREES IN HILLY WOODED AREAS

Physical Features: Gnomes are often mistaken for dwarves. However, gnomes have shorter legs and stockier bodies. They also have strong hands that are often scarred from working in their mines and workshops. Adult male gnomes usually have long white or gray beards.

1

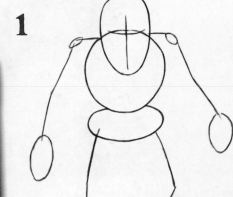

2

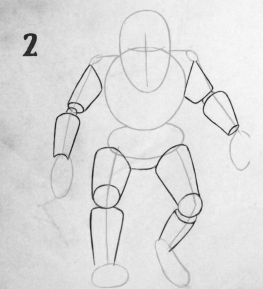

3

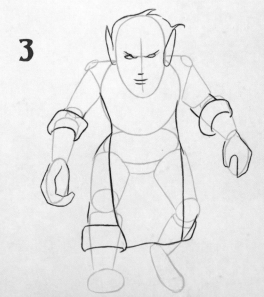

4

5

6

FINAL

WHAT'S NEXT?

After drawing this gnome, try a new drawing that shows him mining for gems or crafting a fine piece of jewelry.

HALFLINGS

Halflings are peaceful people who prefer a quiet life, good food, and the comforts of home. But in spite of their easygoing lifestyle, halflings can be tough. They can overcome many hardships when necessary. Halflings are also very stealthy and can move in total silence to avoid being seen by others.

SIZE: 3 TO 3.5 FEET (0.9 TO 1 M) TALL

HABITAT: DRY AND COMFORTABLE UNDERGROUND HOLES OR SMALL HOMES NEAR LAKES OR RIVERS

Physical Features: Halflings are about half the size of humans. Almost all halflings have curly brown hair. Male halflings sometimes grow bushy sideburns that frame their round faces. All halflings have large, tough feet covered in furry brown hair. They never wear shoes or boots.

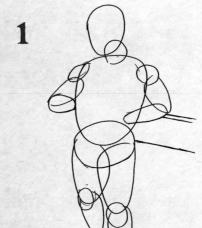

1

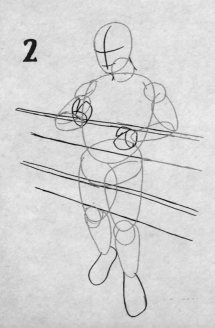

2

3

4

FINAL

5

6

WHAT'S NEXT?

Next try to draw another halfling
as he tries to sneak past a hungry
troll or a goblin hunting party.

DWARVES

Dwarves are expert miners and craftsmen. Few people can match the quality of their weapons, armor, and jewelry. A few dwarves are also skilled at creating powerful magical weapons and armor. Dwarves are a proud and noble people, but they are fiercely private. They don't like answering questions about their families. If offended, they'll simply turn and walk away.

SIZE: ABOUT 4 TO 4.5 FEET (1.2 TO 1.4 M) TALL

HABITAT: AMAZING CITIES BUILT INSIDE HUGE MOUNTAIN CAVES

Physical Features: Dwarves are short but have strong, thickly muscled bodies. They often have lumpy ears and noses. Dwarf men take great pride in their long beards, which they often weave and braid into fantastic designs.

1

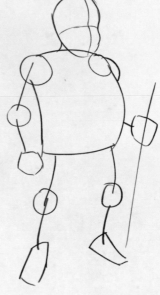

2

3

4

5

6

FINAL

WHAT'S NEXT?

Next try drawing a group of dwarves as they mine for gold and gems deep inside a mountain. Or try drawing a dwarf fighting a goblin or other enemy.

ELVES

Elves are peaceful people with great respect for nature. They also enjoy creating poetry, music, and fine crafts. But when necessary, elves can be fearsome warriors. Their battle skills, magical weapons, and armor are unmatched by anyone. Elves are also very loyal and will always come to the aid of those they consider friends.

SIZE: 6 TO 6.5 FEET (1.8 TO 2 M) TALL

HABITAT: FORESTS AND PEACEFUL MOUNTAIN VALLEYS

Physical Features: Elves look slender and delicate, yet they are quite strong and athletic. They're usually considered very attractive and have long, straight hair. But elves are best known for their pointed ears, bright eyes, and smiling faces.

1

2

3

FINAL

WHAT'S NEXT?

After practicing this elf, try drawing him tracking an orc raiding party through the forest.

6

4

5

DARK ELVES

Dark elves live in a dangerous and violent world. Strong families of dark elves often battle one another for control over their underground cities. Whether using swords or powerful magic spells, most dark elves enjoy attacking and killing their enemies. They often raid cities and villages to steal food, supplies, and people to work as slaves.

SIZE: ABOUT 5.5 TO 6 FEET (1.7 TO 1.8 M) TALL

HABITAT: LARGE CITIES DEEP UNDER THE EARTH

Physical Features: Dark elves have slender bodies, pointed ears, and are usually very good-looking. They are known for their very dark skin and straight white hair. Most dark elves have red or yellow eyes. But in rare cases a dark elf may have dark blue or purple eyes.

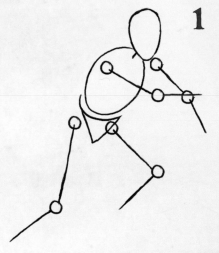

1

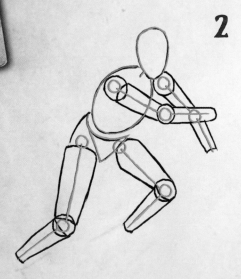

2

3

4

5

FINAL

WHAT'S NEXT?

When you feel comfortable
drawing this dark elf,
try showing another one
fighting a giant spider or
other underground monster.

MERFOLK

Merfolk don't like intruders and fiercely protect their territories. If they see ships in their waters, merfolk will at first smile and motion for the sailors to follow them. But the merfolk's friendliness is just a trick used to lead ships away from their hidden cities. Once at a safe distance, they simply disappear and swim away under the water.

SIZE: ABOUT 7 FEET (2.1 M) LONG

HABITAT: SHALLOW SEAS NEAR TROPICAL COASTS; SOME DEEP INLAND LAKES

Physical Features: Merfolk appear similar to humans from the waist up. They have fair skin, athletic bodies, and waist-length hair. Their lower bodies are like large scaly fish. Their tails end in large fins or flippers used for quickly swimming through the water.

3

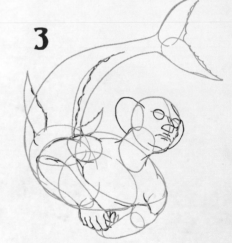

1

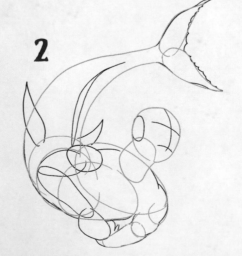

2

4

5

FINAL

WHAT'S NEXT?

Next try to draw a group of
mermaids smiling and waving
at some sailors to get them
to follow on their ship.

25

TREEFOLK

Treefolk are the guardians of the forest. They spend their days protecting trees from being cut down. Treefolk are extremely slow in almost everything they do. However, if they become angry, treefolk can be fearsome. They can easily tear down a large stone fortress in less than a day.

SIZE: 30 TO 40 FEET (9 TO 12 M) TALL

HABITAT: THICK FORESTS WITH MANY TREES

Physical Features: Treefolk look very much like trees. They have thick, trunklike legs and their feet look like tree roots. Their arms and hands look like tree branches and their skin is similar to thick, rough bark. Treefolk usually have large, crooked noses, and some grow beards made of thick vines or moss.

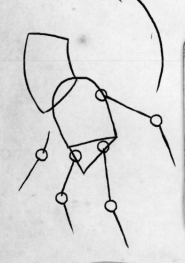

1

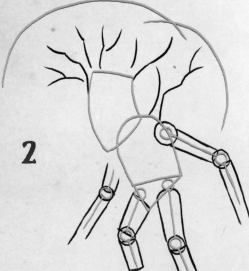

2

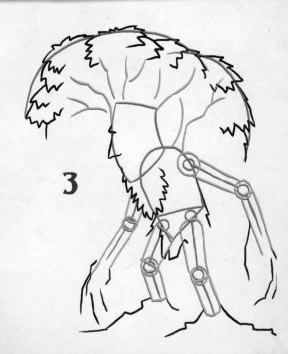

3

WHAT'S NEXT?

Next try drawing a group of different types of treefolk as they gather to meet by a stream or in a forest meadow.

FINAL

4

5

ELVES vs. ORCS

In a time before anyone can remember, elves and orcs may have been distantly related. Both races may have shared interests and physical qualities. But at some point in the past, orcs became corrupt and evil. They became greedy and obsessed with gold and treasures. Over time they grew violent and began killing others, and each other, to get the treasure they craved. They also became hateful of their peaceful elf cousins. Orcs and elves have been mortal enemies ever since. Whenever they meet, they attack each other on sight.

ELVES

SIZE: 6 TO 6.5 FEET (1.8 TO 2 M) TALL

HABITAT: FORESTS AND PEACEFUL MOUNTAIN VALLEYS

ORCS

SIZE: 4.5 TO 5 FEET (1.4 TO 1.5 M) TALL

HABITAT: DARK MOUNTAIN CAVES OR RUINED CASTLES OR FORTS

1

2

3

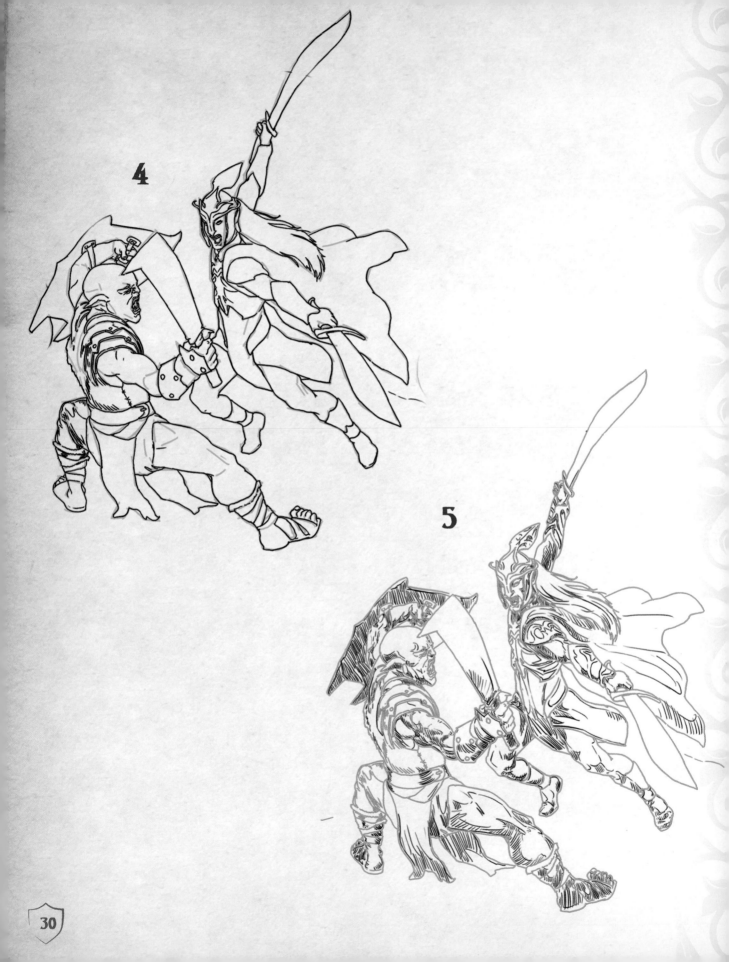

4

5

WHAT'S NEXT?

After practicing this drawing, try to create a large and fierce battle scene. Draw several elves and orcs fighting on a mountainside. Try drawing them in various fighting poses and with different types of weapons.

FINAL

READ MORE

Berry, Bob. *How to Draw Magical, Monstrous & Mythological Creatures.* Irvine, Calif.: Walter Foster Publishing, 2012.

Fiegenschuh, Emily. *The Explorer's Guide to Drawing Fantasy Creatures.* Cincinnati, Ohio: Impact, 2011.

Nash, Mike, (et al.) *How to Draw the Meanest, Most Terrifying Monsters.* Drawing, North Mankato, Minn.: Capstone Press, 2012.

INTERNET SITES

FactHound offers a safe, fun way to find Internet sites related to this book. All of the sites on FactHound have been researched by our staff.

Here's all you do:

Visit *www.facthound.com*

Type in this code: 978491480274

 **Super-cool stuff!** Check out projects, games and lots more at **www.capstonekids.com**